AN OPTIMISM

ALSO BY CAMERON AWKWARD-RICH

POETRY

Dispatch
Sympathetic Little Monster

CULTURAL THEORY

The Terrible We: Thinking with Trans Maladjustment

AN OPTIMISM
POEMS

CAMERON AWKWARD-RICH

A KAREN & MICHAEL BRAZILLER BOOK
PERSEA BOOKS / NEW YORK

Copyright © 2025 by Cameron Awkward-Rich

All rights reserved. No part of this publication may be reproduced or transmitted in any form or by any means, electronic or mechanical, including photocopy, audio recording, or any information storage and retrieval system, without prior permission in writing from the publisher. Request for permission or for information should be addressed to the publisher:

PERSEA BOOKS, INC.
90 Broad Street
New York, New York 10004

LIBRARY OF CONGRESS CATALOGING-IN-PUBLICATION DATA

Names: Awkward-Rich, Cameron author
Title: An optimism : poems / Cameron Awkward-Rich.
Other titles: Optimism (Compilation)
Description: New York : Persea Books, [2025] | "A Karen & Michael Braziller book" | Summary: "Anchored by an epistolary sequence directed to the 20th century poet and activist Pauli Murray, and looking to the work of other trans, queer, and black feminist writers like Audre Lorde, Lucille Clifton, and June Jordan for company and counsel, Cameron Awkward-Rich situate us in spaces intimate and capacious, from lovers' beds to the Gamma Quadrant across the Milky Way"—Provided by publisher
Identifiers: LCCN 2025016360 (print) | LCCN 2025016361 (ebook) | ISBN 9780892556212 paperback | ISBN 9780892556229 ebk
Subjects: LCGFT: Autobiographical poetry
Classification: LCC PS3601.W58 O68 2025 (print) | LCC PS3601.W58 (ebook)
LC record available at https://lccn.loc.gov/2025016360
LC ebook record available at https://lccn.loc.gov/2025016361

The images in "Palinode" appear courtesy of the Schlesinger Library, Harvard Radcliffe Institute, with the exception of the image on page 55, which appears courtesy of the Franklin D. Roosevelt Presidential Library.

Book design and composition by Rita Skingle
Typeset in Ingeborg
Manufactured in the United States of America.
Printed on acid-free paper.

for f, the beloved

CONTENTS

"The Role of The Poet"   3

1.

Long Distance   7
"Cameron, We Know Nothing of Your Inner Life"   9
It Was the Best of Times, It Was the Worst of Times   11
It Was the Best of Times, It Was the Worst of Times   13
It Was the Best of Times, It Was the Worst of Times   14
When Is a Body an Event   16
Trans Study: *Invisible Man* (2003)   18
It Was the Best of Times, It Was the Worst of Times   22

Trans Study: Regarding Lucille's Roaches   25
Lucille's Roaches   32
It Was the Best of Times, It Was the Worst of Times   34
It Was the Best of Times, It Was the Worst of Times   36
Trans Study: *Untitled 4 (Facial Expression)*   38
Odo, Too   39
Palinode   43
Inner Life   73

[Playing Dead]   77

2.

My Life Closed Twice   87
An Optimism   89
Having Been Recalled to Life   91
Trans Study: Uses of the Erotic   92

I Am Deliberate and Afraid	95
It Was the Best of Times, It Was the Worst of Times	97
Inner Life	99
It Was Not Natural	101
For the Record	106
Notes	109
Acknowledgments	117

> ... one of optimism's ordinary pleasures is to induce conventionality, that place where appetites find a shape in the predictable comforts of the good-life genres that a person or a world has seen fit to formulate. But optimism doesn't just manifest an aim to become stupid or simple—often the risk of attachment taken in its throes manifests an intelligence beyond rational calculation.
> —LAUREN BERLANT

> Now I am ready to lay my self down
> on the earth, to listen to the instructions
>
> for how to talk of love & land, to sing
> of home in the horrible years, & to fill
>
> my language, like the stars do,
> with the light, anyway, of a future tense.
> —ARACELIS GIRMAY

AN OPTIMISM

"The Role of The Poet"

There are many kinds of poetry, each
with its own affordances, implicit
politics, posture vis-à-vis the hegemonic
definitions of Literature and Man
and, while I understand the many
arguments against or indifferent to *the lyric*
as a category / ideal / image of some white
someone who, talking at the threshold
of the interior (its dark heart, its bright walls,
etc.), yes, just talking as if to no one
thereby expands their world until it appears
as if it were the world, the self, the
imagination, terms, it should be said,
that never quite (thankfully) address us
but nonetheless press us to their service,
watch us in the grocery store, what was I
saying? Oh, I know all the arguments for
and against my life—

1.

"You know that you are recalled to life?"
"They tell me so."
"I hope you care to live?"
"I can't say."
—Charles Dickens

Long Distance

It's called something
nearly unbearable, the room

on your computer, inside
of which the men shine

with sweat and shea.
They, the men, are passing

another between them
like a lit joint, though they

the burning paper and he
the lips. Plainly, we are

in your bed, watching porn,
though it's purely academic,

everyone merely a student
of pleasure. Except for the boy,

the wet coin, who by now has opened
his second, toothless mouth, swallowing

from both ends, his eyes wide
and then he's gone, vanished

into the body's thicket
and so the men, though

never touching, do—

all four of us, one wooded quiet
carrying his cry. We take

a screenshot, to remember this.
What are we trying to understand?

In the morning, I'll fly home.
It will be months and months

until I am again marked
with your scent.

I'd given up, you know, resigned
myself to the idea of the idea

of desire, the body—my body—
a locked door. Love, if that is your name,

I'm a practiced hand. I'm good
at waiting. And meanwhile,

the sugar maples, miles of them,
flushed and damp between us.

"Cameron, We Know Nothing of Your Inner Life"

I mutter to myself
the reflection of
myself in the mirror
in the morning a kind
of misremembering
I know it's not quite
right the difference
between *not very
much* and *nothing*
the melodrama
of it which I live
for the predictable
narrative entanglements
enlargement of a feeling
until it is the room
one can sing in the cabin
in the clearing
dappled inner light
tulips by the bedside
frozen in
the posture of sleep
her barely-breath lace
against my cheek.
Each morning,
these days, I walk
the path winding
through the woods
behind my chest, knowing
what I'll find but not
what finding it again
will change. I still
grimace in the mirror
like any woman, like
a "true transsexual," though

more and more I am
become estranged from what
the outer gesture means.

It Was the Best of Times, It Was the Worst of Times

It isn't that I was a boy, moving darkly
through the years of my girlhood, still-mute

kernel of future tense scarred by language,
memory, form, etc. It isn't that.

On the phone, my father tells me
he thinks of me as someone daring,

someone who rushes headfirst
into situations that promise pleasure, sure,

a portion of it, but mostly pain, inevitable
as pain is inevitable. I think you'd laugh

at this description, because you know me
now, a me who startles from his skin

if you so much as walk, unannounced,
into the room. *You were always interested*

in your own injury, my father's
saying, *rather than afraid of it.*

Do you remember that morning
when, after sex, you did that thing

lovers sometimes do in the movies?
You moved across my body

like a gardener, stopping to identify
the foliage, what was roses, what weeds.

There was all the obvious stuff, the scars
like anchors on my chest, the tattoos.

But the rest of it—
Anyway, I lied, I was afraid

to tell you how little I cared
for my life for no reason

other than that it was—and will,
interminably, be—mine.

It Was the Best of Times, It Was the Worst of Times

Before we were what we are now, or, as some would prefer it, when we were
latent, a shape moving beneath the blue of that first & longest winter, yes,

before us, I supposed it happened in other people—the wild inside, the violet
blooming of what was never quite desire (*Remember our first attempt?*

It was, frankly, disgusting, wet birds in the closing distance) being thrown
against & through the ice—I thought it would never turn in me

the easy way the others blushed & looked at photographs & whispered
each other's names like they were golden bells ringing in a room

from which I was, perhaps, forever barred. The tragedy of Peter
is not, as you might think, that he remains a child, wavering forever

on the precipice of what we might call love, if we are lazy, a real life.
No, the trouble is he never was a boy, never among the lost nor the living.

He is, let's just say it, a structural position, rather than a puny, tyrant heart.
I'm grown now. Looking back, it seems ridiculous, the gravity I gave him,

his image hovering above me, as if he had in fact been the boy all along—
what can I say? There was a time when we were young

before which it simply hadn't occurred to me, the heart, though I was
of course in thrall to it, though I did of course try desperately

to shut it up. I didn't know yet that it was possible, to be, like that, unmade
& made. That when he dropped me, I wouldn't fall but always fear it.

It Was the Best of Times, It Was the Worst of Times

and we were, of course, two girls trying,
despite the world, to love

each other, though love like anything
can curdle, make you sick.

I was sick of love that night, years after
we lay trembling on the floor

of a room where neither of us lived,
where I touched her for the first time,

touched her not enough to say I knew her
then, only that I would eventually

learn to make her soften in the heat. It's true,
I admit it, I overuse the body—

My body. Her body. The slick light spilling
from the hall. It doesn't matter

what happens to the body. The body dizzy
in the grass. The body tonguing salt.

The body wicked like a shadow, untethered
from the self. I'm not innocent. I came

running when she called. I climbed the steps
to the purple door. I walked right in

to admire the old fantasy, our fantasy
in which I was her girl again

and this was our house, our kitchen
table, our clean bed. It was like a dream

to have the world, the ordinary world
for once. So, yes. I let her have it.

And meanwhile the years between us
washed to gray—

the body blackened like a stone
beneath her—

and it had, therefore, always
been this way.

When Is a Body an Event

Beautiful she says *forgive me but you are so beautiful*
& not wanting to be seen now for what I am dark blot
ruining the idyll smile say *thank you it's ok* it's ok
her hands on my hands this [white] stranger

in the coffee shop & later at the polling station again
so beautiful bloom red inside crabapple shadowing
the heart & later at the coffee shop after hours of reading
attentively look up & there she is the woman

with a changing face *Don't worry* she croons *I think you're
going to get an A* & I don't mean to complain I am
a professor tenured at the end of the university *I'm paid*
I want to want to say as I turn the knob

to the interior roam the scarlet hours
singing gather sour fruit

. . .

Roam the road in the interior
knob the scarlet hours singing
gather by the bucketful bloom
harden into bitter little fists

swallow where no one's looking
high in the magnolia the white
oak when a child no one
could see though had a name

flashing like a coin did not have
the agency to spend lived
an inner life could not bear
the cost pay attention walked

the body to the water of the world—
it was *beautiful a shame so so beautiful*

Trans Study: *Invisible Man* (2003)

> *To be unaware of one's form is to live a death.*
> *I myself, after existing some twenty years, did not*
> *become alive until I discovered my invisibility.*
> —Ralph Ellison

At first, there is a general darkness.
Then, after many hours, a shape

In the darkness, a bright hole
Through which the world is given.

I am right now turning in the hole
Against the general dark. I am

Looking for a pattern I might later call
My life, moments strung like train cars

Rattling the underground. Anything
Could have happened—

Damp air, rosy midnight
Faces, whitened

Grin, fluorescent-lit, boy
Dark and curled

As a comma in the spill
from your fount of naming what

You do and do not see—the boy, I,
Who is pressing my face to the cold glass,

Watching the shadows move, like him,
Across the surface of the earth.

//

Do I have to say it
What I have been? Anything
You roll your windows down
To call me on a quiet night
In a quiet town snow
Drifting in the street-
Light giving form to what
Is otherwise a vague brushing
On the skin I have been
The kindling of that dark a black
Dog dyke-mute in the corner
Monkey muse stud with a huge
Fertile water dead weight to carry
To the finish line I have been
The finish line the threshold vestibule
That marks the win that was not
Mine but me the kill the trophy
Boy in the looking glass girl
In the wishing well gentle buck
Et cetera

//

Yes you named "my"

And "I" became

Inside I

Saw the city move

A shape in the water

You said

And I "was"

A mirror darkly

//

No substance is your first mistake.
No form, the second. The common you assume
No mind, but there is a mind turning like
No machine, little cat patient in her den.
No, the mind is the hole she carves into the solid
World watch what passes through a hole is
Not the absence of form it is where the forms begin—

//

//

In daylight   branches   cut across

Blue opening   untamed sky   I

Am what   you cannot touch

It Was the Best of Times, It Was the Worst of Times

and because I could not drive, because I swore
I'd never, I sat in the waiting room, slick

and winded and helmet-addled.
I was there to start a new life.

On the good days, my high-school
girlfriend would write me letters

describing weekend plans, evasion
tactics, dreams of a future

unloosed from her mother's shame.
And because, by then, I hated her—

or, rather, hated what I became
clenched in her mind's fist—

it was easy to sign the paperwork.
To acknowledge and consent.

Yes. It was my life. I wanted to
tend nothing, least of all my own,

septic mind. It was hardly a decision.
I took the medicine.

I rode, unblinking, into the one body I
would bear. What did I know

about what I deserve?

...

Trans Study: Regarding Lucille's Roaches

with Lucille Clifton

In her childhood kitchen, Lucille is wielding the broom turned blade in her hand. She is becoming, in herself, a murderer.

The roaches, suddenly, a red rain.

She claims to have dreamt this moment *only for a few nights, /and then not much*, though the poems call her bluff. She turns and turns and turns to face—what? Her cruel want of beauty? What she will do? To claim what might be *ours*?

//

Already, the sun is high over a country that is, more than usual, not ours. My friends, nearly all of them, around the table, still tangled in the sheets, making their way through dreams of our *own / particular heaven*.

H has been taking photographs that make us (maybe even me) impossibly beautiful. He says everyone who is not us wants to be here only because they cannot smell the shit wafting through the living room. I look at my friends' practiced laughter—

And yet, I see them, always, this way: *it happens / despite me*
and I pretend

to deserve it.

//

It's clear, of course, that the roaches are—like Lucille, like us—black. The nameless part where anything at all can be done to her. Of course, she'd want to kill, to kill. What is it,

she asks, that makes us faceless to each other? Otherwise, steeped in late-morning light.

//

We come by plane. By plane and plane and plane. We, all of us, copper in the warming sky. We turn down news of *home, / that sad mysterious country*. We spend our government money. Our corporate money. Our American laughter. Our currency.

Twice, the waiter shakes his head, made anxious by our hunger—
"it's too much, I'm afraid, too much."

//

Lucille names this what it plainly is, a global catastrophe. She sees them, the roaches, *bold with they bad selves*. She calls them in our tongue.

Finally, they *turn from us / faithless at last / and walk in a long line away.*

//

At night, we move in one line through the city. P, always in the lead, her glasses black, cannot see herself being seen. The rest of us practice staring back. We become one, dark gaze.

Behind the photographs: Careful lighting. A half-faced cat stalking the veranda. Mosquitos drying red-black on the walls. Nothing will be done to us.

//

Lucille, still in the mute hours of your girlhood. Lucille, walking to school carrying your father's voice. The note written in your practiced hand. *She do not have to pledge to the flag,* he cries, through you, *When it means to her what it means to a white girl, then she may stand.* But perhaps it is inevitable,

you think, cruelty. A child made to speak in the voice of her *family enemy.* We know what your father did. What your country did. *Smiled all the time . . . doing it.*

And Lucille, girl with red rain falling inside you, when given the choice between enemy and enemy, what did you do?   Stood.

You, immediately, stood.

Lucille's Roaches

O winged walker,
motley brood
& brood underneath
the underneath. You,
formidable residual,
derelict carried
to this country
by the dread Atlantic
wind. What did you see
to make but yourself
& yourself? Foul
architect, teeming Queen
of rot. Whereas you
survive. Whereas your death
is an industry. Whereas
on the television
in this century
of television
a woman wears you
as a living jewel,
rubied carapace
on a gold leash.
Whereas *beauty*
was never meant
to be your name—
O harbinger
of harbingers.
O little, unending night.
Whereas *murder*, too,
was never right—
they're just a sound
for what we do
to the dark. O

a sound I fear
is the only sound
I know.

It Was the Best of Times, It Was the Worst of Times

and yet, even so, here we are, at the precipice
of the new century: century of wildfire, century of war

and perfect technology of war, where I live
a happy life, where my love bakes bread

in the morning, where the noon light dances
in her hair and my friends, my friends—

but it's the edge of the century, remember? And you,
sir, are my fifth-grade teacher. A man, not like any man

I've met. I imagine, though can't know, you

alone, weeding the garden of your mind: little rosebush, daffodil,
dogwood tree run amok in the yard, grey cat, green eyes, crypt

in the center where lay your dead and beautiful friends,
your friends who are so far from the life you have now,

where you are, remember, surrounded by children

whom the news of the new president does not touch, not yet,
not, at least, in the labyrinth where they are

the thing at the center, one weeping eye, matted fur, sir—
it's worse than you imagined. The birds outside are singing.

And I understand it now, where you went that day,
when you laid down forever on the floor

of the classroom like you were dead, though you weren't
dead, as we the children flew like so many

terrible, jeweled birds headfirst into the window
of the rest of our lives.

It Was the Best of Times, It Was the Worst of Times

after Ahmaud Arbery

and when I surfaced from the latest
weather—torrent of bad wind

shuttering the blinds, so that I—
or something like me—was lost

and wandering again the stale room
where I fear fear was born, though how

it is impossible to say—when I surfaced
you were talking about children.

A man, barely not a child, was dead.
Murdered, though it was months already

between the scene and that name for it.
The only way I know to outlast history

is running. So that's what I do. I run.
Even though even this action is a pantomime

through which history, we all know it, speaks.
A man, particular, is dead.

And in the general body, the particular now,
I am careful to keep my distance

from the woman who is careful
to smile at me in turn.

When my father did not die, I didn't know.
Nothing happened.

And when he told me, years later,
when the scene found its name,

I found something so like certainty
it must have been. *You don't have to,*

is what I heard him say to me.
Live. You don't have to. Love,

forgive me, for I believed it, believe.
America is more and less itself

than ever. Somedays I run
until my feet go numb,

hum. Somedays I am
the darkest thing I'll see.

Trans Study: *Untitled 4 (Facial Expression)*

This work by John Edmonds was produced by way of the "solarized print" process, a photographic technique that requires extended exposure to light.

Upon first glance, it is difficult to decipher a figure, much less a facial expression. Upon first glance, it is difficult, the figure. Upon first glance, there is no face. Upon first, undecipherable, the glance. It is difficult. It depends on who is looking. We might say: Upon first glance, we are in a dark room. We are behind our eyelids in the room. We are looking, in the dark. The figure before us is also behind the eyelids, their eyelids. It is as if neither we nor they are present to the other, though we are, looking, together, in and from the dark. We look to work out the other's intentions. We cannot. We look. We breathe together inside the room inside. The figure, having been exposed, overexposed, to light, has become like a shadow or a barely lit shape on the midnight lake. For the sake of simplicity, we could call the figure a man, but I will not. We are in the room that precedes all that. The cleavage of this from that. It goes: first darkness, then form. Remember that. Try. If we look too long at the lake what surfaces is the old thought—*when I was a child, when I was a child*—we are thrown back to before, not shame, but shame of shame. We become furious and wild-limbed and kind. We pass the clause between us, a rope tethering, tethering, taut. A poem, we've been taught, though we can't say where, should leave this part out. We should rush from room to bright room so that we can be surprised by what we find. But the figure is still in the dark. They require our stillness. Our black breath. I am afraid, I say to no one, to be like this image. Upon first glance, unreachable. Exposed. When I was a child, there was a figure in the dark. A man. Let's call him that. A man. I was a question. I was a question he answered. I was a question he held and demanded my stillness. Part of me lives in that room, still, though I left it with a new, wretched name. But—and I can say this now—he saw me, the man in the dark, when no one else could see me. When I was, in manner of speaking, difficult to decipher. A darkness before form. He held me. Stilled me. He brought me into the frame. We were two black men there, in the black, the close black, the black from which life, relentlessly, comes. The breath between us was cruel. But I could see him. Him. I could see the sorrow, the rage, the calm water, the father raising his fist, the unnamable quiet of his face.

Odo, Too

Dear Miller,

I wanted to tell you that I've been thinking of Odo, too. Though, Odo later on, in season three of *Deep Space Nine,* once he has found his people, found, in the first place, that he has people—those other changelings who, wounded by history, revenge themselves against what they call *the solids,* the rest of the universe, incapable of change. Of course, members of all species, as far as I know, go through a process of maturation— they are babies then children, they are round then angled, sleek then furred.

Still, as you note, it is different for Odo, perhaps for all changelings— *change* is not the same, precisely, as *growth,* though we can get better at it, change, can come to feel what it is like to *be* a hawk, a shrub, a man, an abstract metal sculpture resting in the center of a room. This, the difference between being and form, is, among other things, what Odo learns when he returns, called by leash or soundless singing, home, where his people form, on the surface of the planet, a great silver sea they emerge from and return to at will—at will an individual, at will a collective shimmer, a motley singularity.

It is difficult to describe what it felt like, what I felt, watching Odo standing on the shore, duty-bound, not to where he (before he *was* "he") "came from" but, instead, to the enemy of his people, his wounded tyrants who want nothing more, it seems, than to govern whatever they find. Odo returns after a while to the station. He requests a room of his own. He fills his room with unrequited flowers, strange particular shapes to explore, to emulate, become. He begins to use words about his life like *joy*.

M, have you wondered, like I have, at Odo's choice, after all this, to remain mostly as he has been—his hair modeled after the hair of the scientist who raised him, studied him for years in a lab believing him incapable of a human life. His face a human face—white, male, though not exactly convincing, something about the smooth of his ears, the cave of his eyes, his gruff bewilderment at rituals of hierarchy and mating. Though, on another hand, we understand (*don't we?*) that we become what we are made to become, approximate the forms of those doctors, those mothers, those lonesome men, brute children who call us unmentionable names, who tell us, not always without kindness, what we are.

Odo, the name he was given, means, he reveals, *nothing*. He is named *nothing*. "Since no one knew exactly what I was," Odo explains, the scientists named him *Odo'ital,* which, in their colonizer's language, "literally means the word *nothing*. Even after it became clear that I was sentient," he goes on, the scientists "kept calling me that. As a joke."

He thinks he is telling this "amusing story" to Nerys, the woman he loves, the woman who brought him flowers, which he placed in the (as you describe it) "futuristic trashcan" he used to collect himself every sixteen hours when he returned to liquid, could no longer hold his human shape. She is dying, he thinks, the woman he loves. She is trapped between forms, crying as he does. What can we offer to ease the passage?

41

"For the longest time," Odo says, "whenever anyone would use my name the first thing I'd think of was what it meant. Nothing." He had been alone. He had known he must change but not what it meant. "I had no family, no friends, no place where I belonged. I thought it was the most appropriate name anyone could give me. And then I met you," he winces, slightly, at his own sincerity. Oh, Brother

tender, take
my hand.

Palinode

The proximities of the archive disperse the feeling of otherwise being consumed by the present and its many emergencies—
    —Jules Gill-Peterson

Reading only with and for transsexuals, I read for my life.
    —Jay Prosser

The Bust by Maysie Stone
1933
and facets - my "id".
The poet
Central Park, N.Y.C.
The Vagabond
Bridgeport, Conn. 1931
The Acrobat
Durham, N.C. - 1931
The Imp!
1931
The "Crusader"
N.Y.C.

Dear Pauli,

I've been trying to write about you for some years now and cannot. Have not been able. Well, other people might say I have been—I've given talks, there's an essay under contract, but I haven't been able, yet, to say what I mean.

Lately, each thing I do is a form of the epistolary. Apostrophe, some particular, impossible you. The problem is, of course, one of audience, address. I cannot have a single thought. From what I can tell, you didn't have that problem. You were, I think, able to hold something like a nation in your head. Still, it must have, eventually, driven you mad, from scene to scene, institution to institution, looking for felicitous language, the precise vocabulary, syntax for making clear what, to you, was always clear. That you were alive.

Anyway, I've been having trouble lately. The sentences either do not come or lie flat or say only what is obvious to say. Life hangs beneath a question.

Dear Pauli,

Am I right to say that, for you, the poet was, at best, a kind of prophet? Not a fortune-teller but, in the biblical tradition, someone who could sense the future looming in the present. Who issues the warning: if we do not change our course, we will be and thus are already doomed.

Dear Pauli,

In interviews, you say that writing was what enabled you to bear your life beneath the question. It was what you did, that is, when no other action was possible. A little valve for when the pressure built. Anger, otherwise, would kill you.

When asked, at 67, at the edge of your fourth (fifth?) career, if you would ever let yourself rest, you said, in short, *I'd be dead if I did.*

In the essay, the one under contract, the one I am already ashamed of, I make arguments, or try to. First, I argue that you understood yourself as living, somehow, in the future—*ahead of myself* is how you put it once, twenty-one years ahead. Second, I argue that this is a trans way of occupying time—living out the future in the present tense, embodying (for others, for yourself) Ernst Bloch's "not yet." It's easy to idealize, being imbued with the sheen of futurity, endless becoming, "longing that propels us," etc. But it's terrible, you know. Or, it is also terrible. People take up all kinds of postures toward the future. Hope is one. Dread. Militarized fear.

I write, if all goes well, to find out what I do not know.

Pauli (Pete) and Alfred

Toni, Betty and Alfred

"An armful"

Pauli & Peggie

Dear Pauli,

Before the war, you had been in love. Not just, that is, experiencing the feeling of love, but held inside of it. Held and then no longer held because love could not see you as you were, a man you tried, for over a decade, to become. Sex was a scene of your impossibility. People interpret this in all kinds of ways (false consciousness, schizophrenia, ego dystonic lesbianism, transsexuality, the disease of reading) and sure. Sure. Me too.

In a prior scene, I am thirteen. I've just finished a novel, *Middlesex*. I am crouching on the blue carpet in my blue room. I am straining to sense how I might too have, secreted inside, the capacity to change.

Dear Pauli,

About you, it was once reported that "[your] errands [were] carefully planned so that [you could] travel in a circle, not wasting time."

In the essay, I argue that although, by the late 1960s or so, you had fallen out of the future, taken up residence in the past/present tense, come to feel history more and more as a series of closed loops, we can sense, nonetheless, in your poems, your photographs, your strained sentences, your trans life preserved in the aesthetic, your still-latent futures given form.

35 Mt. Morris Park, West
New York, N. Y. Apt. 2-C
July 13, 1942

Dr. Joseph Eidelberg   895 Park Ave.
40 West 86 Street
New York, N. Y.   BU-81160

Dear Dr. Eidelberg:

More than two years ago, just after your experimentations with sex hormones had received some favorable publicity, I made an appointment with you to discuss my own emotional problem. You referred me to the clinic at New York Post Graduate Medical School and Hospital, 320 E. 20 Street, and I made one or two visits there.

The doctor who interviewed me was a Dr. Baphan, I think. (Having misplaced the clinic card, I'm not sure of the correct name. At any rate, he advised me to write out my own analysis of my problem and return it to him. A change of jobs and of cities has made it impossible for me to carry out this suggestion until the present time.

Because I am not sure of the physician's name, I am sending you this memorandum. If it was Dr. Baphan, perhaps you will pass a copy on to him.

I am very anxious to have some medical care during my temporary stay in New York. Would prefer private treatment, but would have to know the cost in order to attempt to raise the necessary funds.

If there is no other way out, I shall be glad to attend the clinic. Will you give this matter your consideration and let me hear from you before Friday (clinic day) if possible.

Anything you can do to help me will be gratefully appreciated, because my life is somewhat unbearable in its present phase, and though a person of ability, this aspect continually blocks my efforts to do the things of which I am capable.

Sincerely yours,

Pauli Murray

Dear Pauli,

In 2011, in California, I rode my bicycle for miles to the office of a doctor whose name I do not, any longer, know. He gave me what you, nearly a century ago, had wanted with a kind of fervor I can never muster. I'm not saying it was easy—there had been psychologists and letters and prior attempts and protracted conflict and years and furtive transit and paperwork and endless, deadening talk—but it was possible.

Dear Pauli,

I encounter a thought that breaks, a little more, my heart. You say, finally, that *race and sex . . . are biologically permanent . . . You grow from a child to adult, an alien may become a citizen, [and so on] but where you have a permanent characteristic it is on the basis of one's birth that one becomes a member of that caste . . . It is completely imposed upon one and there is no way that one can escape . . .*

I don't know when this thought, the finality of it, seized you. Was it your admiration of Mary Daly—her writing, her *beautiful tan*? Was it that you could no longer bear hope's disappointment? Was it that you were, in some important way, already dead?

All I know is that, by the end of your life, having discovered no other way, you had become convinced that race, that sex, were closed forms. Pauli, listen, they aren't.

It isn't.

Dear Pauli,

If you were alive now, I suspect I wouldn't so admire you—lawyer, priest, National Organization of Women, acquainted with the president's wife. But, because you are dead, I do.

Of course, if you were alive now you wouldn't be, in every important way, you. I spend my whole life trying to convince my students of this—*our categories have histories*, I say, gesturing wildly with my little nub of chalk. There, at work, I use words like *contingency, discursive formations, rupture, rupture* and yet—

Today, walking with F around our Massachusetts town, I insist, as always, on a circular route—coffee, then groceries, then flowers—for its tender efficiency. Oh, Pauli, how can I help it?

The first, the beautiful thought: *you, you.*

my most natural self, i think

Dear Pauli,

I have been wasting time. Doom is, among other things, why I'm here. Trying to speak to you.

Dear Pauli,

I guess the truth is that I am not brave, do not want to be brave. I want my classes. My students. My domestic poems. I want to move in small circles. I want twenty minutes in the morning, the blue couch, my blue room.

Dear Pauli,

Across the country, across the senates and house chambers and governors' desks and twitter feeds and liberal papers some they is busy legislating sex, race, the people, the human, etc. as closed forms. They are busy, that is, making life impossible always in the name of life. I can offer endless impersonal explanations but I feel it first as numb hand, clenched thought, bird in the throat. What was it you said? *Race [is] the atmosphere we breathed from day to day, the pervasive irritant, the chronic allergy, the vague apprehension that made one,* makes one, *uncomfortable . . . jumpy.*

Dear Pauli,

Even now, I can't say what I mean.

Central Park, N.Y.C.

The poet

Dear Pauli,

I am writing to you because I cannot write. Everywhere there is language, language, language, enumerations of the problem, diagnoses, the problem beginning as far back as I can imagine, farther still. In class, I pace with my chalk, I circle the room, the words—e.g., *neoliberalism, biopolitics, coloniality/modernity, the nuclear family form,* and so on—draw desperate, crooked lines, I say and say and say and what for? Increasingly, I think, there is only one word that might matter. No.

Dear Pauli,

The Acrobat

Durham, N.C. - 1931

The more I look at you the more I am overcome with "an eerie feeling, 'a visceral near-identification' that seems, against my better judgement, that it might rescue me. I [have become] frankly, fixated on this [image of you, you who were] prolific amidst Jim Crow, the fascist American midcentury, the Great Depression, [your] endless dislocation in pursuit of meaningful work, *the atmosphere* of anti-blackness, the deathly race/gender politics of the university, [your] loneliness, [your] . . . unruly mind, the thwarting of [your] trans desires during a tipping point when sex change was heralded . . . as newly possible. Fixated on the question, simply, of how [you] thought under these conditions. How [you] endured the present tense."

Dear Pauli,

No. No. No. No. No. No. No. No. No. No. No. No. No. No. No. No. No.
No. No. No. No. No. No. No. No. No. No. No. No. No. No. No. No. No.
No. No. No. No. No. No. No. No. No. No. No. No. No. No. No. No. No.
No. No. No. No. No. No. No. No. No. No. No. No. No. No. No. No. No.
No. No. No. No. No. No. No. No. No. No. No. No. No. No. No. No. No.
No. No. No. No. No. No. No. No. No. No. No. No. No. No. No. No. No.
No. No. No. No. No. No. No. No. No. No. No. No. No. No. No. No. No.
No. No. No. No. No. No. No. No. No. No. No. No. No. No. No. No. No.
No. No. No. No. No. No. No. No. No. No. No. No. No. No. No. No. No.
No. No No. No. No. No. No. No. No. No. No. No. No. No. No. No. No. No.
No. No. No. No. No. No. No. No. No. No. No. No. No. no. No. No. No. No.
No. No. No. No. No. No. No. No. No. No. No. No. No. No. No. No. No.
No. No. No. No. No. No. No. No. No. No. No. No. No. No. No. No. No.
No. No. No. No. No. No. No. No. No. No. No. No. No. No. No. No. No.
No. No. No. No. No. No. No. No. No. No. No. No. No. No. No. No. No.
No. No. No. No. No. No. No. No. No. No. No. No. No. No. No. No. No.
No. No. No. No. No. No. No. No. No. No. no. no no. No. No. No. No. No.
No. No. No. No. No. No. No. No. No. No. No. No. No. No. No. No. No.
No. No. No. No. No. No. No. No. No. No. No. No. No. No. No. No. No.
No. No. No. No. No. No. No. No. No. No. No. No. No. No. No. No. No.
No. No. nonono No. No. No No. No. No. No. No. No. No. No. No. No.
No. No. No. No. No. No. No. No. No. No. No. No. No. No. No. No. No.
No. No. No. No. No. No. No. No. No. No. No. No. No. No. No No. No. No.
No. No. No. No. No. No. No. No. No. No. No No. No. No. No. No. No. No.
No. No. No. No.No.No.No.No.No.No.No.No.No.No.No.No.No.No.No.No.No.No.No.No.
No.No.No.No.No.No.No.No.No.No.No.No.No.No.No.No.No.No.No.No.No.No.No.No.No.
No.No.No.No.No.No.No.No.No.No.No.No.No.No.No.No.No.No.No.No.No.No.No.No.No.
No.No.No.No.No.No.No.No.No.No.No.No.No.No.No.No.No.No.No.No.No.No.No.No.No.
No.No.No.No.NoNoNoNoNoNoNoNo.No.No.No.No.No.No.No.No.No.No.No.No.No.No.No.No.
No.No.No.No.No.No.No.No.No.No.No.No.No.No.No.No.No.No.No.No.No.No.No.No.No.
No.No.No.No.No.No.No.No.No.No. No. No. No. No. No. No. No. No. No. No. No. No.
No. No. No. No. No. No No. No. No. No. No. No. No. No. No. No. No. No. No. No. No.

No. No. No. No. No. No. No. No. No. No. No. No. No. No. No. No. No. No. No. No. No. No. No. No. No.
No. No. No. No. No. No. No. No. No. No. No. No. No. No. No. No. No. No. No. No. No. No. No. No. No.
No. No. No. No. No. No. No. No. No. No. No. No. No. No. No. No. No. No. No. No. No. No. No. No. No.
No. No. NoNoNoNoNoNoNo. No. No. No. No. No. No. No. No. No. No. No. No. No. No. No. No. No.
No. No. No. No. No. No. No. No. No. No. No. No. No. No. No. No. No. No. No. No. No. No. No. No. No.
No. No. No. No. No. No. No. No. No. No. No. No. No. No. No. No. No. No. No. No. No. No. No. No. No.
No. No. No. No. No. No. No. No. No. No. No. No. No. No. No. No. No. No. No. No. No. No. No. No. No.
No. No. No. No. No. No. No. No. No. No. No. No. No. No. No. No. No. No. No. No. No. No. No. No. No.
No. No. No. No. No. No. No. No. No. No. No. No. No. No. No. No. No. No. No. No. No. No. No. No. No.
No. No? No. No. No. No. No. No. No. No. No. No. No. No. No. No. No. No. No. No. No. No. No. No. No.
No. No. No. No. No. No. No. No. No. No. No. No. No. No. No. No. No. No. No. No. No. No. No. No. No.
No. No. No. No. No. No. No. No. No. No. No. No. No. No. no No. No. No. No. No. No. No.
No. No. No. No. No. No. No. No. No. No. No. No. No. No. No. No. No. No. No. No. No. No.
No. No. no No. No. No. No. No. No. No. No. No. No. No. No. No. No No.
No. No. No. No. No. No. No. No. No. No. No. No. No. No. No. No. No. No. No. No. No. No.
No. No. No. No. No. No. No. No. No. No. No. No. No. No. No. No. No. No. No. No. No. No.
No. No. No. No. no no No. No. No. No. No. No. No. No. No No. No. No. No.
No. No No. No. No. No. No. No. No. No. No. No. No. No. No. No. No. No.
No. No. No. No. No. No. No. No. No. No.No. No. No. No. No. No. No. No.
No. No. No. No. No. no No. No. No. No. No. No. No. No. No. No. No. No.
No. No. No. No. No. No. No. No. No. No. No. No. no No. No. No. No. No.
No. No. No. No. No. No. No. No. No. No No. No. No. No. No. No. No. No.
No. No. No. No. No. No. No. No. No. No. No. No. No. No. No. No. No. No.
No. No. No. No. No. No. No. No. No. No. No. No. No. No. No. No. No. No.
No. No. No. No. No. No. No. No. No. No. No. No. No. No. no no No. No.
No. No. No. No. No. No. No No. No. No. No. No No. No. No. No. No. No.
No. No. No. No. No. No. No. No. No. No. No. No. No. No. No. No. No. No.
No. No. No.No. No. No. No. No. No. No. No. No. No. No. No. No. No. No.
No. No. no no No. No. No. No. No. No. No. No. No. No No. No. No. No. No. No
No. No. No. No. No. No. No. No. No. No. No. No. No. No. No. No. No. No.
No. No. No. No. No. No. No. No.

Dear Pauli,

I am standing before a crowd of people, people I admire, talking incoherently about you, my pursuit of you. What everyone will remember is that I am lonely. Or, that I have formal questions about loneliness, about whether it is a feeling that produces continuity, a desire for continuity, where there might more ethically be rupture.

All day, they come up to me to report that they like what I said about loneliness, which makes me suspicious. Am I lonely? Am I?

Lonely?

My days are crowded with other people.

The Vagabond

Bridgeport, Conn. 1931

Dear Pauli,

I look for as long as I can stand at one particular image. You as young man. You as Pete. You as self-proclaimed vagabond in a leather coat. I go tender for this image. You are young, little brother, so young. This is before Bellevue and the rest home. Before the arrests and the intake forms and your desperate lines. Before you spread beneath the knife, in search of hidden organs. Before the first end of love. Before you are refused and refused and refused and made, I can't help but think, into the bravest thing—black girl, black woman.

(Once, after a talk, someone asked if I thought the name, your name, "Pete" was a biblical reference. Peter, Paul, etc. Honestly, it hadn't occurred to me.)

Dear Pauli,

As far as I know there is no tense, not in English, to describe the shape of time you help me see, the was/will-be. The salted circle. The still not yet.

Dear Pauli,

Your name for her, your first great love, was Pan. Pete and Pan. The boy who would not grow up. The boy who returns and returns to the same house, the same window, though nothing ever is the same. Pauli, the truth is, after all this time, I want him, simply, to have lived. I think this means—shamefully, inconceivably—*I* want to live. To have lived.

Newport (cont'd)

Rocks on the shore

The wave gathe[rs]

The waves at Bailey's Beach

Peggie on the cliffs

Pauli o[n]

And though no word was uttered
Above the tumult of advancing tide,
You came uncalled
And placed your hand in mine.

—Pauli Murray, "For Pan"

Inner Life

Orange light flecked
Crocus purple golden eye
Unreal water
Deep blue knot
Her brief wet eye
Where was before this
Fleeting orange light
Pale magnolia
Downy with buds
Before they break
Open new birds pink
As air there is
No spotlight
To train but for
Sky through the branches
Arms
There are other ways
To enter
Violence delicate breath
The man is saying
Walk through your life
Blue as you have been all
Together and alone

...

[Playing Dead]

F is making dinner

F is moving through the kitchen at a pace

They make purposeful motions

They cut onions

They stir tiny jars of sauce

They become something like a blur

In the distance

I have reached the end

Of the tasks

I have assigned myself

I am putting myself on the shelf

I say, hoping what?

At the rally, I huddle with "the women"

I am meant to be passing

Flyers through the crowd

I let the cold in

I stand impossibly

I ration out my breathing while I

wheel above us in the harsh

December sky

Waking up, I find myself

Somehow on the floor of

The locker room, wet

I am standing just beside

Myself, the shower running

The blood running

From a cut above the eye

I can't say why

I'm naked, kneeling

In her bed again

Her gorgeous scarf

Wound around my eyes

We both use sex, I think

As a scene to negotiate

Our positioning on the grid

Of power, I'm afraid

It can't work

Between us, I am afraid

In greener days, I was made

To touch it, a hand

Around the wrist

I wheel and wheel and

In so doing, I turn my back

The first time it occurred

To me it was a kind of consolation

A line I could cross

At any moment it became

A choice I could make

A different choice

My father could have

Made a different choice

If he wanted to

Suffer and to live

Then, I thought, he was

Choosing it, I wasn't

Keeping him there, suspended

In the fraying air

My hand is numb with hurting

Limp-lying on the tile

The dog's persistent jaw

It is possible, I learned

To occupy the gap

Between sensation and event

To miss, entirely, the pain

I tell him I want to talk

About the accident my brain

Stutters at the thought

Blue coat—

Torn road—

Wet—

With rain—

At the rally, I am meant

To hand out flyers, flyers

I made inviting others

To our work, the work

As yet undefined but vaguely

The work of making flyers, etc

The work of making rallies, etc

The work of sending emails, etc

Of standing with conviction in

Scripted meetings, conducted in

Inhuman grammar so that

Our students might, so that we

Might instead say the words

FREE PALESTINE

And move, somehow

Toward the imagined/unimaginable

That other syntax names I am

Wheeling above myself

A man is shouting

There is laughter in the ambulance

The thought occurs to me

My students are so taken by

June Jordan's conviction

In the generative force

Of language *The idea*

That the word could represent

And then deliver

Into reality what

The word symbolized

I am not so sure

I try to be I try

To speak, though, huddled

With "the women" all I say is

Men in low, conspiratorial tones

Like I know what I mean

The wand of the ultrasound

The doctor's chatter as he rests

Between my knees

Afterward, the long ride home

F when they move in are carrying

A future unimaginable

To me for reasons I can

And have and will

Call "political" but really

The residue

Of ordinary anger

At one's father, one's father

Who could only bear what he could bear

And bore it

It wants to tell you I mutter

I bracket out the baby

Says a word that means *mother* and

Her face turns

The baby says a sound

That means *monster*

And the world drones

At the rally, I huddle with "the women"

I speak the words that mean

I carry June in my pocket, in my as yet

Unreclaimed capacity

For want

2.

But life itself compels an optimism.
—June Jordan

My Life Closed Twice

Liz, I think her name was, the woman
my mother brought me to. We played

cards in her perfumed office: lavender,
tulips, bowl of wax fruit. I was ten

and wanted to die. I don't know why
I'm here again. I lived. Obviously,

I lived. When I was older, but still
a child, not innocent, but foolish,

I looked up from my solitary
suffering. I learned the history

of men. I pointed to a spot
on the map they rendered. I said

then, then, built my common life
in a room at the end.

If it's true, what they say, that poetry
is written with the knowledge of

and against death, that it is
a beacon, a bulwark, then Love,

I confess, I have been no poet.
Outside, a hawk circles overhead.

Four cops circle a woman
dressed all in red. I circle

the apartment as you sleep, happily
in the next room. Just this once

I want so desperately
to be proven wrong.

An Optimism

It is morning. Remember that.
It is morning and the house is quiet,
so quiet that I can, for the moment, set myself
to wandering. I can sit patient at the door.
I can beg and bang to be let in. I am
turning this way and that. I am circling
the hole in the world of my imagination.
Let me in. I am saying the words, predictable
as any key—when I was a child,
when my mother, when the swarm of bees,
when I spent my days in mud among
the worms, rushing down the hill, our flooding
yard, when Hannah's brother, her mother,
when I was too unclean, too wild a thing,
when I was barred from, when I sat alone
in the snow behind her house, pristine,
when, briefly, J and I were, when we
flew darkly down the green suburban
street, when he loved me, or something
in me and I loved the wind between us,
our bloody knees, when I think back, I am
nearly always otherwise alone, though
I never was alone, child of the salamanders,
child of the morning snow, the shamefaced
leaves. All my life, certainly for as long
as I've known I had a life, I was
like the sparrow right now outside
my window, flying headfirst, incessantly
into what must seem, to her, like sky.
All around me people moved and laughed
and seemed, from where I fell,
to understand some silent thing,
some secret word that made itself

no home in me. Aggrieved, the world
of other people. I let it go.

Having Been Recalled to Life

Having once believed
I would be dead was dead

Having been installed in death
in death's position

Having now the power
to extend myself

to own property to be
angry at the man who—

the woman who—

Having for one summer a face
turning toward the sun

Having loved my own kind
Having blood in my mind

Having known I would
walk the valley for a final time

Having been made an example
Having bought a home there

in the example
Having not known

what else there was
to do I suppose yes I

suppose I took it
life like it were mine

Trans Study: Uses of the Erotic

> *we begin to give up, of necessity, being satisfied with suffering and self-negation, and with the numbness which so often seems like their only alternative*
> —AUDRE LORDE

Transsexual is a word my students don't understand how I could want. I get it. I do. No one likes to imagine their heart enabled by capital, power-knowledge, etc. No one wants to know the field, first, as boundary.

Who wouldn't want, instead, to roam?

//

There's a scene that sits, for me, at the center of the story. There, not even the moon is cutting through. I'm outside and can't imagine how my body is moving. It's in the groove, not a good thing, exactly. The groove is something we fall into, a rut, rutting against. Anyway, I am outside the room I am inside, which is perfectly ordinary. The trouble. I used to think there was a series of movements at the end of which: joy.

//

One trouble with *the transsexual* is the history of her description. At the boundary of the field.

A body so alienated from itself it is functionally dead, *a monstrous fetter. He lives only for the day when his "[   ] soul" is no longer being outraged by his [   ] body, when he can function [   ]- socially, legally, and sexually. In the meantime, he is often* [dead to pleasure, to the world outside her head].

//

Take Lorde's *tiny, intense pellet of yellow coloring perched like a topaz just inside the clear skin*. If *yellow pellet* stands for "capacity for joy," then you have to admit that capacity unfolding in and because of war. Likewise, *the transsexual* unfolds.

I is never actually a dead-space, I'm trying to convince myself. It wants only what it is possible to want, which is more than we know. I want the word, I tell you, as a record. A figure for how the barely-possible becomes, through feeling, *a kind of life*.

//

In the field, we lie on our backs and watch the sky moving overhead. We sprawl. We holler. We stand quiet as stones in our own pockets. We wander. We roam. We come back home though in the meantime the description's changed—

//

Tomato. Salt. Bright sting of the needle. Monstera. Buttercup. Breeze through the summer window. *Writing a good poem. Moving into sunlight against the body of a woman I love.* Suddenly, rain.

I Am Deliberate and Afraid

The rain is so loud in our bed
this morning, I cannot stay.
I am trying to recall a dream
in which I couldn't. The rain,
yesterday, destroying roads
(not ours), houses, cars
crouching in the water
like hopeless islands. Useless
men. We talked all night
about how no one can face it,
how we can't; all the art so far
is bad, *disgusting*, I say,
your throat closed against
its easy triumph, selfish
desolations. We talked and then
we went to sleep and I dreamt
I had to leave—

It's like the rain is falling inside
the house. It's so loud, the house,
which is too much, really, for the two of us,
and has no gutters, nowhere for the rain to go,
the deck you love constantly on the verge of flood
and we're supposed to worry, I think,
about the foundation. The house, our house,
has stood, gutterless, for a century,
for nearly two; it's hard not to imagine
that it might collapse just as we got here,
just as we filled it with dark wood and velvet,
with flowers and paperbacks, with our friends,
the laughter of our friends, Hieu singing
"Maybe This Time" with perfect feeling, a little wild
at the end, her hair lifted, briefly, like us, at the roots

by a private wind. *What will you do*
you have tacked to your office wall
with your one wild and precious life?

It Was the Best of Times, It Was the Worst of Times

When walls were raised, we swore we'd be
We swore we'd be a raft inside
A raft inside the whale that we
The whale that we were sovereign of
We sovereigns of though everyone
Yes, everyone was party to
Was party to the angel of
The angel of the pending storm
The rising storm, our little raft
Our sprawling raft inside its eye
Inside its eye where everything
Where everything was calm
O calm against the brackish wall
The bracing wall that was the world
The world that was somehow ablaze
Somehow ablaze with hyacinth
With hyacinth inside the whale
Inside the walls we lived our lives
We lived our lives of mowing grass
Of shearing grass "despite the times"
Despite the times, the children gone
The children gone to future war
The future war of what we made
Of what we made, our money and
Our money and our rage against
Our rage against the hyacinth
The hyacinth, the children
The children who were made to die
Were made to die in futures I
For futures I could not abide
Will not abide I say inside
I stay inside the whale and I
The wail and I we cut the grass
We cut the grass or fail to, so

We failed to and our little plot
Our little plot of life, a raft
Our little plot grown wild, a
Facsimile of wildness,
A wilderness conditioned by
Conditioned by the boundaries
The boundaries of property,
Propriety, the lines drawn in
The lines drawn in the wilding grass
The leaves of grass divided from
Divided from what's not by law
What's not by law the whale, the kids
The hyacinth, o violet fire,
War of life against its end
Against its end we built a raft
We built a raft we thought and now
We thought and now we what? We want
And now we watch, we wait, we watch,
We wait, we watch, we hang up shelves,
We paint our rooms, we dance around
We dance around each other slow
We hear the news we memorize
We memorize the names, the names,
The names we say or don't the lost
Love don't the lost already know
Already know what's rising, love
We rise, we pace, we make, we weather
On inside the whale, I've got
The story wrong, but love I want
I want so much it's selfish yes
It's selfish but I hope we get
To live like this, I hope it isn't
How we die.

Inner Life

Say that you arrive at a clearing—

Say that, this time, the clearing is not a field
        alight—

Say that the clearing is not a brightness
        in the heart of the otherwise
        dark wood—

Say that copper beach, that calla lily,
        that hollyhock, that viola,
        that mangave, that queen
        of the night—

Say that without turning you turn
        to face it, the light-torn image
        of your life—

Say that you enter, dark as you are
        when you were young and then
        when you were no longer young—

Say that you were not lost, the clearing being continuous
        with what it opens—

Say that you are standing now in its center, in you
        there is a music rising you can't
        quite hear, the little hairs of your arms
        dancing in their private weather—

Say that the velvet night, the moonless sight—

        (night embers, crape myrtle,
        geranium, black coral bells)

Say that it seems to extend indefinitely
        in all directions, to sprawl
        across the tenses, *what was, will be,*
        would have been, though
        when you move, it moves with
        and not around you. So here
        you are—

Say that the question is not, in the end,
        whether you deserve it—

        (*what else, what else*)

Say that you carry it—

Say that you carry it, finally,
        past the end of what you know
        you are when you arrive—

        (*dark wind, nightshade, lion's eye*)

It Was Not Natural

with June Jordan, after Alexis Pauline Gumbs

Nothing was born like this. Nothing arose like this from the black dirt. Nothing was shaped like this by the hands of anyone who picked cotton, picked sunflowers, sowed the sweet sky. Nothing natural. We past all that, past that point on the forsaken map. We know what she bears. What scars of our natural, unnatural care. What not given by anything but us. This isn't a story about the fall, no god in the rafters, nothing like that. Just we, what we made—

//

She had been locked in. She had been alone for longer than she had been alive. She was red red red her head, if you could call it that, was bowed. Everything around her was an iron kiln. Everything made her unloved, unlovely shapes. Except, she loved them, the shapes she made, the precise way her breath cut the air. There was a word inside her she could not yet say. There was a world inside her she could not yet shape from the given clay. But she carried it and carried it and carried and it walked with her into red day after red day—

//

Until she stepped outside the category.
Until she had, newly, wings in her hair.
Until she shed her skin daily. Not like a snake,
like the unnamed unnamable she'd became.
Until she became severed from Family,
Family the form that kept her,
kept her *her*, as they sat around the table,
as they feasted, as they honored conquest,
as they talked their way back to shackle and salt.
Until she was a worm in the garden. A jay
in the willow. Until she shed and shed
her paper skin and became, what, alive? Alive
like a stone is alive? Like the whole
breathing, shadowed earth—

//

The cut of sun—

The red iris—

The green, green field—

Running—

She turns to face herself—

She turns to face—

She turns to tenderness—

To tenderness—

The stream running—

Through the green field—

Darkly living—

Darkly brimming—

Intrinsic ardor—

Her her her—

Spilling over—

I—

Like a silver cup—

//

She went on this way.
She went on. This way.
This way, she went on.
On she went. This way.
This way. This way.
This. She went. On.
On. On. Went on.
She went on. She went
on. This way. On. On. She,
went. This way. She went
on

For the Record

I don't know how I began, how I entered
this life of making, repeatedly, the gesture,

of turning the same gold light through the same
window so that it might come to matter less,

the turning, the easy epiphany, which, by definition,
cannot be. I admit there is a certain artfulness

I lack fundamentally and by virtue of my lack
of dedication to the idea a poem might carry anything.

Look at me. I have no boat. I have only the old news
a poem might strike readily like a match

or a like hammer, minuscule
hammering against a dumb bell, me,

who will not sing. Or that's what I said (*didn't I?*)
during the lean years I was fed and fed

but couldn't, for the life of me, I couldn't
swallow. I buried what was given me

in a series of someone else's yards. Readying,
I said, for the winters come and gone. Love,

the poem is not a craft I steer to reach you. Here I am.
For years, my father was always threatening

to take us, my sister and I, to see the Liberty Bell.
It was a kind of joke I didn't understand—

the bell that rang apocryphally for "freedom"
and then, in the long wake, for spectacle

stood in for freedom. All those years
I refused to look at it. I was so bored—

another symbol cracked under the weight
of what it stands for, standing being

its only function. Love, I'm writing to you
from our living room. Our extravagant blue

couch. I'm trying to be unafraid. A little hammer
hitting the same note until I—which is not the same

I—can hear it and, if not exactly believe it is meant
for us, then, nonetheless, live as though.

NOTES

While these poems (and this poet) tend to speak from a somewhat relentless, embarrassed, embarrassing *I, I*—we all know—is an assembly. Below, in order of their first appearance, are the texts/artworks that I know live on the surface of this writing, though I am certain there are others of which I am not yet/still aware.

*

LAUREN BERLANT, *Cruel Optimism*

ARACELIS GIRMAY, "prayer & letter to the dead"

CHARLES DICKENS, *A Tale of Two Cities*

Now, my dear namesake, these innocent and well-meaning people, your countrymen, have caused you to be born under conditions not very far removed from those described for us by Charles Dickens in the London of more than a hundred years ago. (I hear the chorus of the innocents screaming, "No! This is not true! How bitter you are!"—but I am writing this letter to you to try to tell you something about how to handle them, for most of them do not yet really know that you exist. I know the conditions under which you were born for I was there. Your countrymen were not there, and haven't made it yet. Your grandmother was also there, and no one has ever accused her of being bitter. I suggest that the innocent check with her. She isn't hard to find. Your countrymen don't know that she exists either, though she has been working for them all their lives.)
   —JAMES BALDWIN, "My Dungeon Shook: A Letter to My Nephew,"
   The Fire Next Time

LUCILLE CLIFTON, "We Do Not Know Very Much About Lucille's Inner Life"

"[I]nconvenience" draws a membrane across radically private experiences of world-receptivity at the periphery of attention and anything people have to face every day—an ongoing labor situation, a family, a politicized infrastructure they may have been born into, the population they've been assigned to, or other *people's projected fantasies. When is a body an event because of the kind of thing it is deemed to be, as when they walk into a room or cross a state line? What price and what kinds of price are being paid in order to live a life as other people's inconvenient object?...It's inconvenient to bear the burden of a naming you didn't ask for: there is no getting beyond it, only dealing with it as a form of life you live with.*

—LAUREN BERLANT, On the Inconvenience of Other People

Quiet is often used interchangeably with silence or stillness, but the notion of quiet in the pages that follow is neither motionless nor without sound. Quiet, instead, is a metaphor for the full range of one's inner life—one's desires, ambitions, hungers, vulnerabilities, fears. The inner life is not apolitical or without social value, but neither is it determined entirely by publicness. In fact, the interior—dynamic and ravishing—is a stay against the dominance of the social world; it has its own sovereignty.

—KEVIN QUASHIE, The Sovereignty of Quiet: Beyond Resistance in Black Culture

ELIZABETH CATLETT, *Invisible Man*, 2003, Sculpture in bronze and granite, Riverside Park at 150th Street, Manhattan

RALPH ELLISON, *Invisible Man*

Slavery did not transform the black female into an embodiment of carnality at all, as the myth of the black woman would tend to convince us, nor, alone, the primary receptacle of a highly profitable generative act. She became instead the principal point of passage between the human and the non-human world. Her issue became the focus of a cunning difference—visually, psychologically, ontologically—as the route by which the dominant modes decided the distinction between humanity and "other." At this level of radical discontinuity in the "great chain of being," black is vestibular to culture. In other words, the black person mirrored for the society around her what a human being was not. Through this stage of the bestial, the act of copulating travels eons before culture incorporates it, before the concept of sexuality can reclaim and "humanize" it.

—HORTENSE SPILLERS, "Interstices: A Drama of Small Words"

ROBERT HAYDEN, "Those Winter Sundays"

Lucille Clifton, "[at last we killed the roaches]"

Lucille Clifton, "shooting star"

Can beauty provide an antidote to dishonor . . . ?
    —Saidiya Hartman, "Venus in Two Acts"

What kind of schools and what kind of streets and what kind of parks and what kind of privacy and what kind of beauty and what kind of music and what kind of options would make love a reasonable, easy response?
    —June Jordan, "Foreword," to Civil Wars

Lucille Clifton, "[when i stand around among poets]"

Lucille Clifton, "[after the reading]"

Lucille Clifton, "the beginning of the end of the world"

The fact of domination is alterable only to the extent that the dominated subject recognizes the potential power of its own "double-consciousness." The subject is certainly seen, but she also sees. It is this return of the gaze that negotiates at every point a space for living . . .
    —Hortense Spillers, "Interstices: A Drama of Small Words"

Mary Jane Lupton, *Lucille Clifton: Her Life and Letters*

Lucille Clifton, "note to my self"

Lucille Clifton, "[cruelty. don't talk to me about cruelty]"

Lucille Clifton, "[won't you celebrate with me]"

Mr. D'Amato, to whom I have owed an apology

In what I am calling the weather, antiblackness is pervasive as climate. The weather necessitates changeability and improvisation; it is the atmospheric condition of time and place; it produces new ecologies . . . what must we know in

order to move through these environments in which the push is always toward Black death?
  —CHRISTINA SHARPE, *In The Wake: On Blackness and Being*

JOHN EDMONDS, *Untitled 4 (Facial Expression)*, 2018, Photograph, Solomon R. Guggenheim Museum, New York.

EVA HAYWARD and CHE GOSSETT, "Impossibility of That"

MILLER OBERMAN, "Odo"

IRA STEVEN BEHR and ROBERT HEWITT WOLFE, writers. *Star Trek: Deep Space Nine*, season 3, episode 14, "Heart of Stone," aired February 6, 1995.

JULES GILL-PETERSON, "Feeling Like a Bad Trans Object"

JAY PROSSER, "A Palinode on Photography and the Transsexual Real"

PAULI MURRAY, The 'Life and Times' of an American Called Pauli Murray. Pauli Murray Papers, personal and biographical, photograph album, ca.1919-1950, n.d. MC 412, 24vf. Schlesinger Library, Radcliffe Institute, Harvard University, Cambridge, Mass.

Everywhere in the descriptive document, we are stunned by the simultaneity of disparate items in a grammatical series: "Slave" appears in the same context with beasts of burden, all and any animal(s), various livestock, and a virtually endless profusion of domestic content from the culinary item to the book... That imposed uniformity comprises the shock, that somehow this mix of named things, live and inanimate, collapsed by contiguity to the same text of "realism," carries a disturbingly prominent item of misplacement. To that extent, the project of liberation for African-Americans has found urgency in two passionate motivations that are twinned—1) to break apart, to rupture violently the laws of American behavior that make such syntax possible; 2) to introduce a new semantic field/fold more appropriate to his/her own historic movement.
  —HORTENSE SPILLERS, "Mama's Baby, Papa's Maybe: An American Grammar Book"

PAULI MURRAY, "The Prophetic Impulse," in *Pauli Murray: Selected Sermons and Writings*, edited by Anthony B. Pinn

"First Black Female Priest Also Lawyer, Poet," *Ashbury Park Press*, March 18, 1977

"Pauli Murray 'I Seek Only Discovery': The First Negro Episcopal Priest Has Spent a Lifetime Doing What Others Got Around to Later," *The Baltimore Sun*, April 24, 1977

JACK HALBERSTAM, *In a Queer Time and Place: Transgender Bodies, Subcultural Lives*

JOSÉ ESTEBAN MUÑOZ, *Cruising Utopia: The Then and There of Queer Futurity*

ROSALIND ROSENBERG, *Jane Crow: The Life of Pauli Murray*

VIRGINIA WOOLF, *Orlando: A Biography*

PAULI MURRAY, Letter to Dr. Joseph Eidelberg, July 13, 1942, Pauli Murray Papers, Box 4, Folder 71

PAULI MURRAY, "Oral History Interview with Pauli Murray," interview by Genna Rae McNeil. Southern Oral History Program Collection, February 13, 1976.

PAULI MURRAY, Letter to Mary Daly, August 11, 1971, Pauli Murray Papers, Box 94, Folder 1650

PAULI MURRAY in New Hampshire, November 1955, Franklin D. Roosevelt Presidential Library.

PATRICIA BELL-SCOTT, *The Firebrand and the First Lady: Portrait of a Friendship: Pauli Murray, Eleanor Roosevelt, and the Struggle for Social Justice*

PAULI MURRAY, *Song in a Weary Throat: Memoir of an American Pilgrimage*

Cameron Awkward-Rich, "Looking for Pauli, Pauli Murray's Trans Poetics"

Eve Kosofsky Sedgewick, "Queer and Now," in *Tendencies*

Heather Love, "Emotional Rescue: The Demands of Queer History," in *Feeling Backward: Loss and the Politics of Queer History*

Pauli Murray, *Dark Testament: Poems*

www.instagram.com/fjp_umassamherst

June Jordan, "Problems of Language in a Democratic State"

June Jordan, "Nobody Mean More to Me Than You And the Future Life of Willie Jordan"

June Jordan, "Foreword," to *Civil Wars*

June Jordan, "Intifada Incantation: Poem #8 for b.b.L."

June Jordan, "Notes of a Barnard Dropout"

Emily Dickinson, "[My life closed twice before its close]"

You think your pain and your heartbreak are unprecedented in the history of the world, but then you read. It was Dostoevsky and Dickens who taught me that the things that tormented me most were the very things that connected me with all the people who were alive, or who ever had been alive. Only if we face these open wounds in ourselves can we understand them in other people. An artist is a sort of emotional or spiritual historian. His role is to make you realize the doom and glory of knowing who you are and what you are. He has to tell, because nobody else in the world can tell, what it is like to be alive. All I've ever wanted to do is to tell that.
    —James Baldwin, profile in *LIFE* (May 24, 1963)

Aaron Smith, "Boston"

Jean Valentine, "Door in the Mountain"

Claudia Rankine, *Don't Let Me Be Lonely: An American Lyric*

We have arrived at the necessity for developing an understanding of class relationships that takes into account the specific class position of Black women who are generally marginal in the labor force, while at this particular time some of us are temporarily viewed as doubly desirable tokens at white-collar and professional levels.
  —Combahee River Collective Statement (1977)

Audre Lorde, "Uses of the Erotic: The Erotic as Power"

Radclyffe Hall, *The Well of Loneliness*

Harry Benjamin, *The Transsexual Phenomenon*

—Transsexuality frightens
us, it confesses how much beauty matters
to life.—
  —Stephen Ira, "The Only Place"

Audre Lorde, "New Year's Day"

Zal Batmanglij and Brit Marling, The OA, season 1

Mary Oliver, "The Summer Day"

Walt Whitman, "Song of Myself"

Rick Barot, "On Gardens"

Justin Phillip Reed, "When I Was a Poet"

Taylor Johnson, "self/hood"

GWENDOLYN BROOKS, "The Sermon on the Warpland"

ALEXIS PAULINE GUMBS, *M Archive: After the End of the World*

JUNE JORDAN, "The Difficult Miracle of Black Poetry in America: Something like a sonnet for Phillis Wheatley"

& so to tenderness I add my action.
      —ARACELIS GIRMAY, "The Black Maria"

ACKNOWLEDGMENTS

Many thanks to the editors of the following for first publishing poems included in this collection, often in slightly different forms or under different names:

Academy of American Poets: "My Life Closed Twice"
American Poetry Review: "It Was Not Natural," "Inner Life," "'Cameron, We Know Nothing of Your Inner Life,'" and "For the Record"
Arc: "When Is a Body an Event," "It Was the Best of Times, It Was the Worst of Times," and "It Was the Best of Times, It Was the Worst of Times"
BOAAT: "Long Distance"
Feminist Formations: "It Was the Best of Times, It Was the Worst of Times," and "Trans Study: Uses of the Erotic"
Kenyon Review: "'The Role of the Poet,'" "It Was the Best of Times, It Was the Worst of Times," and "It Was the Best of Times, It Was the Worst of Times"
POETRY: "Lucille's Roaches," and "An Optimism"
Transchool Vol. 2 (Co-Conspirator Press): "Odo, Too"

Additionally, "Trans Study: *Invisible Man* (2003)" was commissioned for *Invisible to Whom?: Poetic Responses to Invisible Man*, a March 2023 collaboration between the Studio Museum in Harlem, the Schomburg Center, and Cave Canem; "Trans Study: Regarding Lucille's Roaches" was commissioned by the 92nd Street Y for *Joy and Hope and All That: A Tribute to Lucille Clifton*; and "Trans Study: *Untitled 4 (Facial Expression)*" was commissioned for *Going Dark: The Contemporary Figure at the Edge of Visibility* by Ama Codjoe in her role as 2023 Poet-in-Residence at the Guggenheim.

This book, and I, exist because of so many others. Thanks, in particular, to everyone at Persea Books and especially to Gabe Fried, for his enthusiasm, care, and patience. To the librarians and other workers at Harvard's Schlesinger Library, and especially to Mimosa Shah, for their kind assistance with the images from the Pauli Murray Papers. To the Lannan Foundation, for financial support, for living room. To Michelle Neely and her colleagues at Connecticut College, whose invitation to speak at the 2023 "Illuminations of a Horizon": Beaver Brook Symposium on African American Literature recalled something to life in me. To my students in "Poetry and/as Black Feminist Thought" and "Trans/Queer of Color Thought" at UMass Amherst, for their willingness to risk tenderness and rage, to learn alongside me, which has taught me so much.

To Hanif, Sam, Hieu, and Ari, for reading a draft, for holding me to your deadlines, for inviting me out of the shell of myself. To Nick, for steadiness, for change. To Danez, Fati, Alison, Nate, Paula, and everyone else in my poetry family. My family.

To Frances, for travelling with me past a horizon.